Why Would You Leave Me?

a memoir by

Leslie Harper Worthington

Finishing Line Press
Georgetown, Kentucky

Why Would You Leave Me?

Copyright © 2026 by Leslie Harper Worthington
ISBN 979-8-89990-351-9 First Edition
All rights reserved under International and Pan-American Copyright Conventions. No part of this book may be reproduced in any manner whatsoever without written permission from the publisher, except in the case of brief quotations embodied in critical articles and reviews.

Publisher: Leah Huete de Maines
Editor: Christen Kincaid
Cover Art: Keenan Worthington
Author Photo: Aryn Davis
Cover Design: Elizabeth Maines McCleavy

Order online: www.finishinglinepress.com
also available on amazon.com

Author inquiries and mail orders:
Finishing Line Press
PO Box 1626
Georgetown, Kentucky 40324
USA

Contents

I

Your Own Story 1
Why Would You Leave Me? 2
Did She Cry? 3
Was I Four or Five? 5
Compartmentalized 6
Long Island Poet 7
Tears 8
We Are Seven 9
Guilty Faces 10
My Drunk Uncles 11
Kindergarten on the Down Low 12
Stand Any Place 14
Fridays After 5:00 15
Papaw's Passing 16
Appalachian Assimilationist 17
Harper 18
Sanibel Island 19
On This Day of the Solar Eclipse 20
Nostalgic Notes 21
A Mother's Luck 22
Lesser 23
Doubt 24
Giraffe 25

II

The Day Before the End of the World 29
Crash 31
In an Instant 32
A Curt Pause 33
Survivor 34
Only Sixteen 35
Parentification 36
Broken 37

Hibernation 38
A Prayer for the Truck Driver 39
That Voice 40
But Then There Were Books 41
Books in Bloom 43
Try 44
An Issue of Abandonment 45
Pertinacity 46

III

That Anchor 49
Time Machine 50
And So She Fed Me: To My Grandmother 51
Late Dreams 52
Alzheimer's Ode 53
The Clock Test 54
Funerals Pass 55
The Colonel's Request 56
Lake Side Burial 57
Fools Rush In… 59
These Attic Things 60
Splitting the Sword 61
Remembering: For Papaw 62
My Grandmother's Hands 63
Happy Siblings Day! 64
Missed Opportunity 65
Separated 66
Namaste, My Sister 67
Ladybugs 68
Journeying 69
Blue 70
Unreliable Narrators 71

Acknowledgments 72
With Gratitude 73

To My Grandfather
"Papaw"
William Clifford Harper
(1912-1978)

I

Your Own Story

Telling it feels
maybe a little indulgent
even self-absorbed
possibly misremembered
like when the cat fell
through the porch
or a bird knocked
on the back door
Even so, perhaps
someone benefits
from knowing

Why Would You Leave Me?

Wee intruders
often mournfully
left
in maternity wards

Would-not-be
Mothers
drifting off
alone

But you swaddled, bundled, and carried me home

Two short months
then
I'm squalling
all alone

A foundling
left
to find

Left
to continually
imagine
what you could have meant

Did She Cry?

Sometimes bundles of joy
are just secrets
that bellies won't keep kept.
Rejected at conception so
no one planned the layette.

I imagine she cried
when she left me.
She may have imagined
my life passing before her eyes
and if I would take many roads
not traveled by.
I wonder if she doubted,
if she would ever come back.

I like to think she thinks of me
on my birthday
and maybe the anniversary
of that day sometime later
when she left.
I imagine she sees
All the difference.

Maybe she remembers how I cried
but there's no indication of it.
We just went our separate ways.
What do newborn babies know
of ceremonies and certificates?

Blood can sometimes run
a bit thinner than water.
Mothers don't always bear a mark
to signify.
Sometimes they walk the earth
just looking like any other.
And you're forced to wonder
as you wander
not looking anyone in the eye.

A lifetime of love
doesn't always fill the depression
your mother left.
Years and years hence,
you realize
Bastard babies are born
with broken hearts.

Was I Four or Five?

Following a yellow butterfly
floating above the Honeysuckle
waiting on the green glider
always too excited to stay in the house
I wanted you to see me first.

Was I four or five
when you came to tell me
you weren't who I thought you were
I wasn't who I'd been
our parents were really Grand?

Would I come away
where I'd have
another Mother
and the baby sister
I'd so wanted?

Now, you said,
I could call you "Dad."
I can't remember
who decided
I wouldn't get to go.

I do remember—
I stopped waiting for you
on the porch.

Compartmentalized

Sometimes
discarded children
don't feel real
as if born
without permission
cancelled
Possibly
defense mechanized

Long Island Poet

Snow covered the beach
in that strange land
where my parents lived without me
and the sky was gray.
Scented beads of bubble bath
filled the tub where
my mother, who wasn't mommy,
bathed me.
Thirty-seven miles from Whitman,
I had evidently been born there.
At five, I didn't know him yet
or them.
Like Cats in Hats and Blue Birds too,
I knew what they didn't
like the boy out of the cradle knew.
How fitting that my first memory of her
should be a poem too.

Tears

I grew up without
Tears. My mother gave me some
Things to cry about.

We are Seven

She ferried,
labored, delivered, then
took her leave of us.
Relinquished.

I know
you each exist
as much as
I.

Even if
we're not supposed
to talk about
You.

I know because
there are rooms where
we're not supposed
to talk about
Me.

Guilty Faces

I know why
you couldn't love me
Guilt
across my forehead
Shame
stamped on my cheek
My face
reminds you—
all the little faces
all my twins
left some place

My Drunk Uncles

I learned to discern
Drunkenness
by the age of five or six.

I had many uncles
all but one a drunk.
Some to the point of homelessness,
some only occasionally so.
I had strict instructions
from my grandmother.
When they could come in
and when they must sleep
on the green front-porch glider.

I liked some more so than others.
Those I liked I often allowed in
even when I knew I shouldn't,
Uncle Teddy
with his guitar and lovely voice.
Sometimes I made Uncle Slim
stay outside
even when I knew
he was only a bit tipsy.

My grandmother would
always give them a good meal,
and my grandfather'd
pass them a dollar
when she wasn't looking.
Their visits amounted to a little excitement
every now and a bit,
and provided a brief occasion
when I called the shots.

Kindergarten on the Down Low
Portsmouth, Ohio 1967

It's been said,
we learn everything we need to know
in Kindergarten.

On the first day of attendance
in that most sacred of institutions,
dressed in navy, pleated skirt, ruffled blouse,
white knee socks, and black patent mary janes,
much more 1950 than 1967,
I walked the two blocks to school with my grandmother.

When we arrived,
my grandmother asked to speak with my teacher in private,
so I was directed to the "library,"
a shelf of books
on the far side of the room
under the only window.
There were books!
Books I hadn't read.
But I soon made a horrifying discovery.
Those books were wordless!
Silent!

Pictures of that ever-famous Dick and Jane
and Spot and Puff, who doesn't love Puff?
But no words.

There must be some mistake.
Book in hand, I raced to the teacher.
The authorities must be alerted.
A wordnapping had occurred!
My grandmother was mortified by my enthusiasm,
as she often was.

My first teacher looked at me
as if I were without doubt—a freak.
What on earth would a five-year-old need with words
her expression would follow me into college,
what would a woman need with knowledge.

When the other children began to arrive,
we were allowed to play
in the "centers" before class began:
a tiny kitchen with wooden stove and sink,
cradle with baby sound asleep
and across the room, building blocks,
the big, red, heavy cardboard kind that look like bricks.

I hit the bricks.
Boys were building a fort.
I was told I could play
but only if I would be the nurse.
Girls were not allowed to point their fingers like guns,
and certainly not girls dressed in ruffles and patent leather shoes.

A girl in flowered mini dress and blue moccasins,
who introduced herself as Donna,
snickered and mumbled "no wonder" when I told her my name.
Boy-ISH, at best.
She asked what I thought I was doing on THAT side of the room.
Forts were not where girls played.

She'd already gotten the lay of the land.
We hadn't been there
even one whole day!

By the time I walked home a few hours later,
I was indeed a much more educated child.
Just the first day of my kindergarten instruction, and
I had learned
not only did my grandmother dress me funny,
but my name was quite ridiculous as well.

Also they can call things whatever they want,
library—book—play
but it doesn't make it so.

My most important lesson though—
girls live within certain parameters, and
smart ones need to learn to live on the down-low.

Stand Any Place
      1969

My Grandmother said
God didn't need to see
us in church.
But I needed to see church.
I needed to feel freedom
walking the four blocks alone.
I needed to stand up
and say my piece.
"Little Lamb Who made thee?"
I needed to sing the prophecy,
I'd fly away one day.
I needed to see Sister Haddie
preach her piece from the pulpit
every Sunday.
I didn't have to hear her say
what a girl could be.
I could see her,
see her shout the gospel
Sing the Grace.
God didn't fly away
from that little church with me
but Sister Haddie did.
I saw her say
I could stand any place.

Fridays After 5:00

On Friday afternoon, he'd come home from the shop earlier, and we'd walk up 7th Street, cross over to 8th and travel till it turned into Gallia Street, what we'd call Gal-yuh, headed to the Public Library, a Carnegie Library, I'd later discover. But first we'd stop at Richard's News, an official Hallmark Card Center. He'd walk the narrow isle to the magazines across the back of the store. I'd round the corner to the toys and work through the coloring books. He'd pick one, don't guess I ever knew what kind, then find me with mine. He'd pay, and we'd be off to the next stop, the Grand Event. The Library, the noblest building I was ever inside. Sandstone façade, columns three stories up, a portico, what looked to me like a crown on top, with 1906 inscribed, older than him by six entire years. Steps and steps and steps to get inside. Then all marble and stained glass. Stacks and stacks. Up, up, up, to the stained-glass dome. I called it lemon-lime. Yellow and green with flowers and designs. Breath was a struggle in its presence. The sun would shine through reflecting flowers on the floor. I once found it in a book, Domes of the World, alongside ones from Spain and France. This was our church, his and mine, no one went there with us. We'd enter in total silence and split up, me to my section in the basement and he to his, where the books were much more refined. We'd meet back at the desk to checkout our stacks. I could get only as many as I could carry in my pink and white polka dot satchel, the one a redheaded boy would later throw out a school bus window. I'd stack my treasures on top of the coloring book. But not headed home yet, first, next door to Crispie Crème for treats. Mine, white powdered heaven with cream inside; his, black coffee. Then we would sit across the table and read our books in the quiet on Friday after 5:00.

Papaw's Passing

My grandfather's skin
was brown
But I am
beyond the pale
a blonde product
of the genetic blender
I knew who he was
even if others
were not supposed to

"Supposed to"
an inconspicuously
potent phrase

Even then
he was searching
those Kentucky hills
for his stolen heritage
fossils
stones
ancient stories
crafting monuments to it
harboring dreams of resistance

At home
he called himself
"Indian"

Appalachian Assimilationist

My blood flows like a silent river,
through the wide Appalachians.

Here the O, and sometimes A, turns to ER and
the R turns up in the wa(r)sh where it's not supposed to be,
sounds prance round like they ain't got no manners,
and my grandmother says to me,
"Don't listen at that talk.
Yourn's everwhat it's s'ppose to be,"
as if it were pre-ordained.

But I am bilingual
because I don't walk the mountain terrain.
If I can't play the banjo or the mouth harp
as my Papaw did,
how will I ever harmonize or
decide who I am?

Though never my home,
the mountains sing to me.
But all I know is what I can pay to see.
I walk back still pretending.
Like Boone, I search for my elbow room.

They were the backwoods Scots-Irish-Cherokee,
but I am a true-blue Urban Appalachian.

Harper

Celtic Harps populate
My Appalachian Heritage
Many Musicians
Comprise my Clan
All taking up Strings
Of Diverse Design
Not Heavenly Harps
As much as
Mountain Mandolins

Sanibel Island
    1974

New moon morning
low spring tide—
walking
Sanibel beach

Gathering shells
with my grandfather
whole dollars
stars, completely intact,
GIANT conch
buckets of tulips
junonia jewels

Some still squirming with life
"Put those back,"
he said.
But that didn't help.
Now all more precious
in scarcity.

**On This Day
of the Solar Eclipse**

I am reminded,
one so long ago,
my sixth-grade year,
school almost
out for summer,
all of us,
Mrs. Horton's science class,
gathered
in the school yard
with our handmade
eye gear—
Waiting.

Twelve, the awkwardest year,
some curious Creature,
not a child,
not a grown-up,
Eclipsed the you
You know.

That day,
we all stood
looking up,
waiting for the sun
or something like it
to reappear.

Nostalgic Notes

Where did you go
that summer day
in Sylacauga,
suddenly that song
on the Chevy's radio?

"Does a song ever take you back?"
"Put you right there?"
"Another place, another time?"

At 12,
I had no idea.
She liked to forget
when I was a child.

Fifty years later,
I know that Nostalgia
Exactly.

Yes, I go there,
that day
that day we were confidants
every time I hear,

Is this your way to hide a broken heart?

"Mona Lisa"
Nat King Cole

A Mother's Luck

"You're lucky,"
she said.
"Everyone tells you
you're smart."
"All I ever heard was
'You're pretty.'"
She never
said either
to me.

Lesser

They wanted me
to be ashamed
of myself.
To see
how much Lesser
I was.
But no one
would stoop to
tell me why.
Without WHY,
I refused to
Comply.

Doubt

When all the wide world
is the stage, but your set part
has yet to take shape.

Giraffe

"Long neck,"
My grandmother's
term of endearment.

At twelve, I was
"All arms and legs,"
"Gangly," maybe.

Tall was obviously
all wrong, and I was
taller than the rest.

At school, they'd
taunt me with
"Giraffe."

Maybe, they assumed
I'd cry, but
Giraffes are silent.

Instead, Giraffe
befriended me,
became my totem.

Now, tall was elegant and wild,
unique and powerful, with
lashes to-die-for.

II

The Day Before the End of the World

Once Upon a Time,
the day before
the end of the world,
I became defiant.
I began to misbehave,
to disrespect,
to insert my logic.
This can happen at sixteen.

My grandmother, as always,
demanded her logic, her way,
which was THE way or the highway.
For once, I said
"My way, no, my way…"
She almost didn't know how to act,
as Southerners say.
It was a first
from me to her.

I wanted to spend the summer away…
away from the limits
of my grandparents' old folks home,
away from nowhere to find a first job,
away from no way to hang out with friends,
away from "no way you're taking the car,"
away from being watched,
away from being held in one spot.

It was a month in the big city
with the "real" parents,
people I barely knew—
the month before school started back.

I promised I'd come home.
She doubted me.
She fought hard.
I fought harder.
My grandfather settled it.

Talking was rare for him,
but what he said happened.
I would stay.

I wrote the "I'm sorry" note,
then hid it away in her purse.
I'd be home in a month.
Everything would be the same.
She'd find it tomorrow.
Everything would be forgiven
tomorrow.
I was sure of tomorrow.
A month wouldn't matter.
So many more the same.

Early the next morning,
they left without me.
Sometimes,
the end of the world
comes unannounced.

Crash

I can only
imagine
the impact
Glass in skin
Metal on bone
I stepped out
just in time
She folded
Compartmentalized
He never
stepped again
Everything
forever altered

In an Instant

Then
He was gone—
"In an instant,"
they said,
"on impact."

The one who
continually said,
without ever saying,
"You are loved."
"You are safe."
"You are real."

A Curt Pause

I want to believe
Death is only a curt pause
in conversation

Survivor

Walking, talking,
standing
through each breath
limbs and lungs
intact

While they crumbled and cracked

the disobedient child,
unharmed, stepped out
a Volcano of
Guilt

Only Sixteen

Now you pay the light bill
Bring in the clothes from the line
Peel the potatoes
Bake the chicken
Carry the bed pan
Sometimes,
if you make it
to the bus
you go to school.

When all the grownups
are gone
all but one, the one
who can't get out of bed,
who do you become?
When you are sacrificed?
When they leave you
not entirely alone?

Parentification

There's a word for it,
My childhood,
"Parentification."
When the adults
assigned,
maybe by God,
to care for you,
a Child,
abdicate their duties.
They don't
abandon you
exactly.
They don't
just make you
care for yourself.
Somehow,
without even realizing it,
you start taking care of them.
They say, the experts,
this makes you
forever different,
changed from the child
you were and even
from the adult
you would have been.
There are signs and symptoms.
It's not quite a disorder,
more a personality:
fiercely independent,
overly responsible,
obsessively organized,
always in control.
Thank goodness
they named it.
Now we're real.

Broken

While I breathe
I hope
but broken pieces
fall hard
I pocket them
and march on.

Hibernation

There's a certain kind of tired
that a cat-nap can't fix
that a good night's sleep
won't repair

Hibernation is required

When
your eyes won't clear
a perpetual fog
surrounds your brain
and you can't carry
the clothes on your back

When
you discover
that heavy load
is you

A Prayer for the Truck Driver

They said he was twenty-two.
I don't know much else about him.
Maybe he was asleep at the wheel
or merely distracted for the moment.

If I still prayed,
I'd say a prayer for the truck driver,
so young and now
so guilty.

The best portion of a good man's life
lost to preoccupation, inattention,
recklessness or perhaps
daydreams.

That Voice

Is common sense
the voice of God?
That quiet little voice
of logic in your head?
The One
you often smother
because you don't like
what it said?

But Then There Were Books

I was lost
but books found me.
They were my only
Survival,
the way I made it
through the loneliness
and fear,
the fear she'd die
and it would be my fault.
Even if it wasn't,
where would that leave me?
Sailing down the Mississippi alone?

They were ignoring
I wasn't actually
Grown.
Without her,
where would I go?
Homelessness loomed over me,
like so many orphans in story books
or worse.
Houses where I wasn't welcome.
Houses that could have already taken us in
but didn't.

I remembered the way I felt
when she'd say, "I didn't take you to raise"
and when she'd remind me
not to forget
the homeless kittens
shoved in sacks,
tossed in Rivers
or her threats to leave me
on the side of the road.
She was the one
who kept me.
What would anyone else
care?

But in the books,
where all the little orphans
found homes,
It didn't matter
if no one wanted me,
I didn't even
Exist.

Books in Bloom

Books are the mind's Roses.
They wildly bloom within us,
blossoms of fancy.

Try

What do you do
when the hand
dealt you doesn't
match your mind—
Who you dream to be?

When the world says
you're a girl or a boy,
but you know you're
really someone
in between?

When you know how smart
you really are,
but the words you see
aren't where they're
supposed to be?

When you can't stand
or walk or run,
but you know
you could
play anyway?

When something's wrong
inside
but a mother is all
you've ever dreamed
you'd be?

Maybe you try
you're version of things.

An Issue of Abandonment

When I asked
why
she would leave me,
she said,
"He made me."
both times?
"It was you or
him."

She wanted me—
Not to forgive her—
But to say
that made sense.
That's what I would have done.

Pertinacity

Back then,
I survived
day to day
only by
minute
Pertinacity.
Now
I scream
at the dead,
"I was a Child!"

III

That Anchor

Striving to be
what never was
on hand—
Someone to hold
off the storm,
tuck me away,
safe in the hold—
treasured Cargo.

Stanchion of Steel,
holding the ship
steady,
while the headwinds
endeavor to drag
us off course—

Weatherworn
through time and struggle,
still striving to be
that Anchor.

Time Machine

I want to build
a time machine
so I can be the agent
of my own design.

I'll get there just in time
to kill the now-me
by compromise.

I'll leave
Graffiti messages
on bridges
I'm sure to find.

I'll hunt
myself down
and whisper warnings
in then-me's sleeping mind.

I'll befriend myself.
For once I'll say,
"Do the right thing!"
And make it just for you.
I'll teach myself
all the things I never knew.

I'll write mauve lipstick
messages on speckled mirrors:
"Lovely"
"Smart"
And "Kind."

Then I'll travel home
and relax in the real-me
having been my own best guide.

**So She Fed Me
To My Grandmother**

She couldn't hug me
when I fell and bloodied my knee,
so she fed me
biscuits and eggs scrambled in an iron skillet.
She couldn't say "I love you,"
so she'd bake me a cake.
When my puppy died,
barely six weeks old,
we had homemade vegetable soup and cornbread—
my favorite—for a week.
When she passed
this past summer,
I gained twenty pounds.
No matter what I eat,
I feel no solace from my grief.

Late Dreams

I dreamed last night
that my grandmother came
from the grave to see me.
She was wearing the blue apron
she always wore when she made biscuits
and standing over my bed
the way she would
when I was going to be late for school.
Her hair looked the way it did
when I was about eight.
She wasn't deathly creepy.
But she was frantic that I warn my sister.
"Tell her not to have the surgery!
Tell her it won't help!
Tell her it's dangerous!" she said,
in that doomsday way
she had said so much.
She made me promise,
and I did over and over
as I searched for the cat.
I woke to a clap of thunder.
Struggling with the covers and
stumbling down the hall,
I was frantic to get to the phone
to call my sister.
I was halfway to the kitchen
before I remembered.
she died last fall.

Alzheimer's Ode

Born before you were ready,
never quite yours,
five years passed before
I saw your face.
Awkward explanations
for this foundling,
somehow not as pretty,
odd and studious,
even harder
for you to claim me.
But not unlovable or
incapable of love.
Most of life
lived without you,
the judgmental gaze
too severe.

As time passed,
I started to wonder
whether you even saw me.
You'd talk politely as if
to a stranger.
Then someone would say,
"your daughter"
and you seemed to remember
something you never knew.
Now so many youthful stories
pour forth,
Memories I never knew.
The magic words must be spoken.
Then the gaze transforms. And
you've forgotten to remember
why you left me all alone.

The Clock Test

Can you draw a clock?
Eventually, she couldn't.
I wonder if her mother
could.
They could drive.
They just didn't know where
they were going.
My mother would disappear
for hours
to be found miles from home
confused by foreign parking lots.
Eventually, you take their keys,
but Grandmother searched
stray purses at holiday dinners
and stole cars.
There comes a time
when they don't know you
and eventually when they
don't know themselves.
I wonder if,
eventually,
I won't know me.

Funerals Pass

And when she
was really gone,
I barely noticed.

She'd never really
been where I was,
never much a part
of me or mine
or Life.

I was invited,
asked to bring
my family,
but it seemed
such a lie.

I couldn't bring myself
to pretend she
was my mother
not even
for a polite goodbye.

The Colonel's Request

In the final morphine haze,
his lungs hardening like cement,
oxygen barely able to weave
through the bronchial crevices,
my father demanded his Colt Mustang.
"I'm going out back to end this!"
He couldn't even sit up,
but he would hold command
until the final Punch Out.

Lake Side Burial

This is not a poem about Water
because poems rhyme,
you always said.

But this one won't.
I can't make it.
The sounds won't come out of air.
The words won't form rows.
They are all just vowels and consonants
flying through my head
like memories of walks through the pasture on the farm,
or sitting on the floor next to you,
zipping and unzipping the zippers on the pant leg of your flight suit.

You did not go gentle into life.
For right or wrong,
you raged against the mold that you were given.

For years, I reached for you.
Finally caught hold.

A leap of faith that landed me on a sounding board
garnered me not just a distant hero
or even the father I always dreamed you'd be
but a close friend.
No rhymes reveal the magnitude of this gift of time.
Yes, I know this isn't a poem,
just the words I was able to crash land on rocky terrain.
This is just a sentiment as we bequeath you
not to earth but to water
because you were a man of water and air
not the earth
to lay long in a box of wood.

I won't go to the church yard
or sit by a grave.
I'll paddle the lake
or sit by the shore at sunset.

I'll think of you wandering the waters,
exploring the depths,
like Ulysses, a soldier seeking distant shores.

And I'll remember you and me
on the deck
watching the sun slide slowly into the lake
admiring how the rays are a bit more pink today,
then going in after dark
when the bugs start biting
to watch an old cowboy movie
or talk of books and birds,
and always stay up past my bedtime,
like I once dreamed we would.

Fools Rush In…

Decades ago,
too late for me,
my parents wed
on April Fool's Day.

I always wanted to ask,
"Who fooled who?"
But they have since
died and divorced.

Maybe we should
move the holiday of Love
from Valentine's
to April First.

Actually, most marry
on Labor Day
Labors of Love, I suppose,
or maybe just for the alliteration.

I married shortly
before Halloween.
You can guess
how that turned out.

These Attic Things

An Oriental
Jewelry Box
filled with long
discarded treasures
secured by
a broken latch
Tarzan first editions
ragged covers
broken spines
Bongos, Banjo, Tambourine
the music of my forefathers
Glass Gun
silver capped
rainbow candy beads
eaten a hundred years before
the Grandfather Clock
pendulum broken
over time

Among these ancient
forgotten
not quite castaway
things,
Memories of lost
Family resides.

Splitting the Sword

Walking through the woods,
he gathered fronds of fern,
with his pocketknife
gently dug the root
along with the viridian blade.
Tenderly, he placed it
in a jar of water.
The kitchen windowsill
its second home.
Eventually, it migrated to
a petite purple pot of soil
and took up residence
on the back patio
where it commenced to grow.
Over the years,
it grew and grew.
Long after he was gone,
she cherished it
above all others
because he had raised it
like he raised their own.
Then she too was gone.
We split the Sword fern
into three,
one helping for each.
My third grew and grew.
Years and years passed until
a startling Christmas Frost
surrounded it.
Five decades
lost in a shameful second.

Remembering
For Papaw

Will those I tell remember?
The ones you never met
not just remember but reveal you
tell their children and grandchildren
keep you living if only by reminiscing
memories of my stories of you
I must write to remind them
so you are never forgotten
never lost from thought
eternally living somewhere
not just a picture in a crushed box
or a name on a withered piece of paper
someone who lived and
did all that the living do
who walked around in my life
someone worth remembering
when my remembering is through

My Grandmother's Hands

I look down to see
my grandmother's hands
on the kitchen counter,
measuring out
the necessary amount of flour,
stirring the batter
for the lemon bars
I've promised to bake:
Same purple patterns
as the blood moves
through to chubbing fingers,
similar tiny spots—
white and brown,
even a few as red as cherries.
Her face stares back
from the mirror each morning.
Eyelids droop like pale curtains
over open windows,
still a sliver of blue sky beneath.
My father's mouth
smiles at the resemblance.
Generations may pass,
but familiar tokens
dwell in our DNA.

Happy Sibling Day!
     April 10

Happy Sibling Day!
Those proclamations
make me think less revelry
and more Rivalry,
but I'm sure that's not
what's meant.

So I wish a Happy Day
to all, always far away,
to some I've seen but
only once or twice,
and to the anonymous ones
I'm still convinced exist.

All said and all done,
and all that
Water under the Bridge.

Happy Day to all
who somewhere may
Still live.

Missed Opportunity

I always feel weird
in Texas.
I know that's where
she left you,
where you're all
supposed to be.
Every time,
I feel
a missed opportunity,
like I should be
combing through old records,
calling a PI,
as if there's a chance
my DNA is nearby.

Separated

Siblings—
stairsteps,
Irish twins,
born a year apart,
meant to share a crib,
steal each other's toys,
walk to school together,
become best friends.

But she left us—
a world apart,
torn across time zones,
raised by mothers,
neither one our own,
lost to each other,
before we even
knew our names.

When we finally
found each other,
we searched
for the familiar,
but we couldn't
make anything
the same.

Namaste, My Sister

Like a shadow—
I can't lose the thought
that in my loneliness
you were only corners away.

I always felt
there was someone else,
someone who should have
belonged to me.

But lies kept us apart.
Family made us strangers.

I think I may have
heard tell of you
in family whispers,
a secret gem
denied me.
Maybe I heard your name
or maybe I dreamt you,
imagined you,
wove you out of scraps.

A big sister—

I named my dolls after
what I thought was you,
my daughter too—
after the fantasy
we were denied.

After so many yesterdays,
I have set down my anger.
Now, it is enough
to feel your presence
across the distance
and know you are happy.

Namaste, my sister.

Ladybugs

They say
Ladybugs are lucky
and Clover
Acorns
A Penny found
All so
Tiny
because luck
comes in miniature.

The burden
of life
briefly mitigated
by a speck of
mythical resistance.

Journeying

We are all
continuously
wandering
toward
some
infinite
completion

Blue

When you're color-blind,
all the shades of blue,
are just blue.
Maybe black is really navy.
What could be orange is perhaps red.
And all the shades of pain
can look like hate to you.

Unreliable Narrators

We are all
the Unreliable Narrator
of our own existence:
Telling yesterday stories
Remembering our perspective
Casting Villains
Stepping into Heroes
Righting dialogue
Edifying
The End.

Acknowledgments

Grateful acknowledgment is made to the following publications where the listed poems first appeared:

"Appalachian Assimilationist." *Belle Reve Literary Journal*, Summer 2015.

"Friday After Five." 2025 Short Prose Poetry Award (3rd place). Alabama State Poetry Society.

"Harper." *Expressions*, 2024.

"Ladybug." *Expressions*, 2023.

"Long Island Poet." *Eastern Sea Bards Poetry Anthology*. Local Gems Press, 2024.

"My Drunk Uncles." *Cardinal Arts Journal*, 2025.

"Papaw's Passing." 2024 Otis Dees Poetry Award (4th place). Alabama State Poetry Society.

"Splitting the Sword." *South Carolina Bards Poetry Anthology*. Local Gems Press, 2023.

"Stand Any Place." 2025 A Childhood Memory Award (2nd place). Alabama State Poetry Society.

"Time Machine." *Cardinal Arts Journal*, 2015.

"Your Own Story." *Cardinal Arts Journal*, 2025.

With Gratitude

I have many people to thank for helping me with this collection. Thank you to my children and grandchildren who patiently listen, read, and discuss my poetry: Sydney, Jacob, Keenan, Anna, Haylee, Ivy, Kaiden, Wren, and Violet.

I especially want to thank Keenan Worthington for photographing the cover art, Wren Gaines for posing for the little girl in the woods, and Anna Leckie for helping to create the lovely book cover.

I must also thank Gloria Bennett, Wesley Bishop, Tabitha Bozeman, Kaitlin Hoskins, and Kristin Kelly for their time and attention to my poems, their excellent advice, constant encouragement, and belief in me and my quest.

Leslie Harper Worthington holds a PhD in Southern Literature and recently retired after a 40-year career in higher education as both an English professor and academic administrator. She is a recipient of fellowships from the Georgia Institute of Technology (Brittain Fellowship), the Center for Mark Twain Studies at Elmira College (Quarry Farm Fellowship), and the Key West Literary Seminar.

Dr. Worthington is the author of *Cormac McCarthy and the Ghost of Huck Finn* (McFarland, 2012) and co-editor of *Seeking Home: Marginalization and Representation in Appalachian Letters and Song* (University of Tennessee Press, 2016), a volume nominated for the C. Hugh Holman Award. In addition to numerous scholarly articles, her poetry and fiction have appeared in publications ranging from *CHEST: The Journal of American College Chest Physicians* to *Proud to Be: Writing by American Warriors*, *The South Carolina Bard Poetry Anthology*, *Stonepile Writers' Anthology*, and *Sugar Mule Literary Magazine*.

She is the author of two poetry collections: *Why Would You Leave Me?* (Finishing Line Press, February 2026) and *Lingering: A Poet's Journey through Literary Landscapes* (North Meridian Press, forthcoming Summer 2026).

Now residing on Lookout Mountain in northern Alabama, she devotes her time to writing, traveling, and enjoying her children and grandchildren. A lifelong writer, she has returned in retirement to her creative pursuits, using poetry to explore the complexities of human experience and to forge honest, lasting connections. Dr. Worthington writes to remember, to understand, and to leave behind words that may endure.

Facebook:
https://www.facebook.com/profile.php?id=61579681103920

LinkedIn:
https://www.linkedin.com/in/leslie-harper-worthington-94372313a/

Website:
https://www.leslieharperworthington.com/

www.ingramcontent.com/pod-product-compliance
Lightning Source LLC
Chambersburg PA
CBHW030056170426
43197CB00010B/1544